Out West

Michael O'Lear y

Out West

The Cultural Society

Out West
ISBN 9780999491294
© Copyright by Michael O'Leary
all rights reserved

Published by The Cultural Society
culturalsociety.org

for Esther and Cyrus
"Our hearts are restless…"

The beginning of my career in the nuclear power industry coincided with the discovery of 84 trillion cubic feet of technically recoverable gas in the Marcellus Shale of the Appalachian Basin. Gas prices dropped precipitously in the wake of increasing production. With no carbon tax in the foreseeable future and a seemingly endless supply of natural gas, it became cheaper to build and operate a gas plant than a nuclear plant for the first time in the United States. By 2015, analytical work in nuclear power had become scarce. I agreed to take a six-month field assignment at a plant on the central coast of California to expand my skill set and maintain job security. The high cost of living in California along with the low per diem negotiated on behalf of contract engineers made it challenging to visit my family in Chicago more than once a month. Having grown up in Michigan and having lived my entire adult life in Chicago, I knew little about California other than a few visits to San Francisco. As I was putting on a hazmat suit in preparation for entering the reactor building while gazing out at the big blue Pacific, it was hard not to question the decisions that led to my temporary exile. Outside of work at the plant, I had nothing but time and California to explore. Most of the poems in this collection are born of that wandering.

First night heading out west
        pulled in late
to a roadside motel in the middle of Missouri.
Hoping to get somewhere west of Denver
        the next day,
somewhere deep in the mountains,
but feeling creaky at dawn,
        so took a run
before the long drive to loosen up.

Newly leafed soybeans all along
        county road Z.
No cars except for the sound of the interstate
        a mile or two off.
Roadside gravel and uncut grass,
        the whole landscape
bathed in the light vapor of late spring,
the bottomland steambath of midsummer
        still a month away.

I had the wide Missouri to cross,
lunch at Arthur Bryant's to look forward to,
        the rolling hills of Kansas after that,
and a flutter of two white butterflies
        right in front of me
ascending and descending in a double helix
past a honeysuckle bush
        so thick with blossoms
I stepped into it just to catch a whiff.

On the coast of California
        I would dream
of mornings like this,
        the soft humid air
and how well it carries the perfume
of manure, honeysuckle, new grass.

Just west of Bakersfield outside McKittrick
a sign read "next gas 60 miles"
but I hadn't seen a station in nearly fifteen.
The tank had over two and a half gallons,
enough to make it to Santa Margarita, so I pressed on
into the blonde hills of the Golden State.
I'd spent the night before in the Mojave desert
with a sleeping pad on the desert floor
and woke up at dawn to find a dun-colored horizon
fading into a haze pixelated with starlight
and a bull that had been lowing the night
before up in the hills and now bluffed a charge
until I walked away. It was only later
when I was looking at a map that I realized
I'd been climbing up the coastal hills and there was
no other way over but the winding road
I'd been on. Bakersfield had pulled at me in ways
I hadn't expected. Bleached, a little shitty,
but not broken like towns in the Midwest.
I bought some fat dates and oranges from a man who looked
more like a factory foreman than an orchard keeper.
As not a single car descended while I climbed
the hills and burned my fuel, I devised to walk
back down to McKittrick with my oranges and dates.
But no need. I made it to the top and coasted
down the lonely hills to Santa Margarita
where I watched kids in gingham getting gas
kissed by the afternoon sun and a summer
to look forward to. They seemed happier than kids back
in Chicago. Who knows? As I continued to
the coast I only thought about getting there
to see the ocean. But the mountains crowded
me in as I approached Avila Beach, a town known

for humpbacks and RVs. There it was. Perhaps more
modest than I expected. More blue. Less unruly.
Perhaps like Italy, or parts I'd seen in movies.
The mountains ran right up against the Pacific
and the horizon was crowded by a low bar
of fog. I'd expected something like the freedom
you find in Montana or western Kansas, all
that raw space and nothing to clutter the landscape,
but what I discovered in Avila Beach was
as unfamiliar as the coast of Crete. I walked
out on a wooden pier, pelicans and people
everywhere, and rising behind me the Coastal Range
turning everything vertical. Fog shrouded
nearby Pismo Beach, but this little sinus
shone like a blue jewel. When I reached the market
at the end of the pier I couldn't believe all
the mammals there swimming and yelling beneath my feet.
Sea lions I was told. And sea otters and seals.
And humpbacks coming soon, just in time for June gloom.

Long after chowder, small talk
among strangers.
Flicker of NBA finals
synchronized in rows
of hanging tulips and snifters.

Fog thick as cotton. No moon.
Light more confusing than the grey dark
that opens like a cave.
Motels and cafes closed.
Wanderer on the street, nowhere to go
except the beach.

Thunder of surf, hiss of retreat,
distant screech of seabirds.
Mountains out there;
black hill, hidden lagoon.
Between two cypresses, what is
and what isn't.

I vaped
the shit

out of
my rig

today:
drip tip

tootle
poofers

fogged in
smurf cake

my all
day vape

All the motels and campgrounds on the central coast
were occupied through the second weekend of June
so I drove up to Berkeley on a Friday afternoon
to hide out at my sister-in-law's and make the most

of a quiet weekend while she went up to Siskiyou.
I rarely left her place except to see a movie
about the life of Brian Wilson and how cruelly
his father treated him all the way to Malibu

where he stayed in bed for three years watching tv.
On my way back to the apartment I bought bread
and cheese and a dozen green-striped figs I thought were bred
to look like little watermelons, so juicy

and sweet, the seeded pulp like jam, though slightly lurid.
I first visited Berkeley back in '93
when it brought to mind Ann Arbor with lemon trees
but that's all I could compare it to as a tourist.

I wondered then if I'd end up in Berkeley
thinking it was a quiet place like Port Huron
where I could read and live cheap and get a room on
the bay, not realizing if I wanted cheap

I'd have to look around for a little town
in Missouri or a tower in south Milwaukee
where I could gaze at Lake Michigan for free
and walk over to a corner deli renowned

for their crispy panini, which being
so cheap, you always grab a few more to go.
I drove to San Francisco a few years ago
with my family to do a little sightseeing.

Blackberries fattened in big patches agog
for plucking up near Twin Peaks. Cats stalked the labyrinths
at Lands End and skulked among the inhabitants
of the Greenwich steps hidden by fig leaves and fog,

the fog that floats like silk scarves in the Sunset District
and lassos an old Thai restaurant at the bottom
of a hill in the Haight where we stopped for tom yum
before going on to Golden Gate Park slicked with

enough mist to baptize don Quixote's bare crown
and permit the gilded Buddha's halo to gleam
at the approach of a few late afternoon sun beams
that graced the park as the carousel was closing down.

I went to Alcatraz as a boy and came
away with a prison-striped painter's cap labeled
"Escaped from Alcatraz" after the fabled
prison break gouged out by spoon and concealed by paint.

Later that day we took a cab to a special
store devoted to Dungeons and Dragons to look
for metal miniatures and a new rule book
governing campaigns and combat on the astral

and ethereal planes. I wore that hat back
home until it grew too filthy for my mother
to tolerate, but I never found another
I liked as much, the thin plastic coated brim cracked

as if decorated with a dingy filigree.
Alcatraz! Sanctuary for cormorants!
Sullen gatekeeper to the half-formed currents
of counterfactuals sweeping escapees out to sea.

after EM

Through the gloom the surf surges
    nothing to do
        about the circumstances

would've been better to be
    a medieval serf
        than constantly chase work

pay the bills to survive
    find an ally
        only to say goodbye

nothing done but paperwork
    in the daily churn
        nothing gained but debt

professional
    bereft of purpose
        scavenging what's left

vanity to imagine
    otherwise
        to want more than waves

Slow and spooky tremolo
      followed by two tom hits—boy,
            do they sound good with the solo.

Hi-hat against the guiro
      through the patter, through the Oooos,
          all the way through the intro.

Open the door, sweep the porch,
      shake the dust from your shoes.
          Sundown glows like a blowtorch

somewhere beyond Malibu
      where it's easy to confuse
          land for water, black for blue.

Fog drifts across the lot
        like blooms of jellyfish
                through an estuary.

There is an hour between
        the witching hour and now
                when the night has ended.

Somewhere between "Rose Darling"
        and Lester Young blowing
                "These Foolish Things" over

the ocean below, morning comes.
        Time flows but also drips.
                What happens in between

slips through like trying to
        recall the color of
                a hallway in a dream,

or finding cellophane
        inside a waste basket
                emptied the night before.

Out West

It was so much the end of things   I.
       I found myself in California free
of most ideas. Here I am,
with no place to stay, at the end
of the recession on a field
       assignment out west, where the fog
that nourishes the hanging moss
can't slake the coastal range so pale beneath the ceaseless sun.

All frequencies of visible
       light ricochet through the cerulean
penumbra of the exosphere
and meet the eye identically.
Only the mind can know the blue
       of the sea and infer trajectories
of light from ideas of beauty.
The change from frame to frame is relative; what does not change

is the pursuit of what is beyond
conception up through canyons grey with fog
then powder blue, a secret word,
       a dream remembered darkly now.
           The shore appears and disappears,
       the scent of fennel on the wind
climbing the mountain's spine to a nuclear power plant
perched on a cliff above the Pacific where it all ends.

A neutron hits uranium
　　　and splits into krypton and barium
releasing three more neutrons
and all the binding energy
described by $E = mc^2$.
　　　The neutrons split more ^{235}U,
releasing particles and heat
until each fission event branches into an avalanche

of energy which is transferred
　　　to water flowing past the core to drive
the turbine, and the turbine turns
a huge magnetic tube around
a coil of copper wires. The change
　　　in magnetic flux through conductive wire
induces current through the coils,
a surge of free electrons to conduct a flow of charge.

The speed at which electricity moves
is not the speed of drifting electrons,
but that of electromagnetic waves
　　　interacting with particles,
　　　　　imparting energy from one
　　　electron to another back
and forth like metal balls in Newton's Cradle through the wire,
like the quick signal of your voice pulsing through waves of air.

Out in the open ocean ground
       swells grow as wind presses the surface of
the sea and fetches a sea state
of waves. Columns of plankton drift
offshore in coastal streams and when
       a wave passes through, krill orbit the crest
and trough without a net advance.
Deeper below, they only oscillate laterally.

As swells approach the shore, a reef
       or sandbar slows the wave down, steepening
the crest, which, freed from the constraint
of other water, breaks away,
exceeds itself in an inverse
       expression of bathymetry and falls
in a curtain back to the sea,
a breaking hyperbolic umbilic catastrophe.

To feel the pull, the sudden rise and curl,
what thunders over and under the swash
of froth and foam, to see the width of it
       fizz into mist above a sea
              marbled with spume and feel again
       the pull of gravity, the roar
thundering over, pressing a momentary silence
under that churn where nobody knows the way up or down.

A flock of piping plovers tracks
  the contours of the shoreline back and forth,
a vector field shifting in time,
and long-billed curlews deftly step
in that uprush to probe the swash
  for shrimp or pluck a sandcrab from the flats
like sushi on a geta tray.
Sea lions nose out of the foamy surf and pelicans

slope soar the lip along the crest
  of breakers while low crowds of cormorants
arrow out to sea stacks offshore
where humpbacks breach to feed on eel,
jacksmelt, and mackerel; colonies
  of gulls descend the wave-cut benches of
Obispo tuff and Monterey
formation in a frenzy for the carcasses of fish,

oblivious to forces gathering
in rock along the fault three miles offshore
expressed as seafloor scarps or sudden slips
  releasing centuries of strain,
    shaking the earth, shaking the sea,
  shaking the very air we breathe.
This is the end of things, the end of finding something new,
all of the disappointment and failure consumed in blue.

It happened on a Friday night,   2.
          early spring, sidewalks still sloppy with slush,
nowhere to go, nothing to do,
so went up to my girlfriend's room
as her dad watched tv downstairs
          when she pulled out a Ouija board for fun
and asked, despite my skeptical
demur and nervousness, the spirits to divine our fate.

At first the answers came in waves
          of yes or no. She would end up out west
as a photographer. My fate
arrived in letters. B-E-R-K-E-L-E-Y spelled
a destiny where I would write
          a book O-N-G-O-D. How would it be received?
E-A-R-T-H-S-H-A-T-T-E-R-I-N-G. The spirit then
departed, leaving me to wonder what I would do next.

Earth shattering's a phrase I might have used
when young but *On God* is an odd title
for a pretentious kid from the burbs
          familiar mostly with the Beats,
                    punk rock, and Nietzsche, but not with
          medieval treatises where I
might've gleaned a tone, assuming the words came from the exchange
between her and me and not the daemon we were speaking with.

Next day, I woke up late, depressed.
      Should I simply wait for my fate to guide
my actions or should I somehow
prepare myself? Why should I try?
I was a teenage atheist
      without a clue; what did I know about
theology? Should I go out
to Berkeley with the goal of writing something about God

or would it happen anyway
      despite intentions to do otherwise,
like Oedipus, who when he heard
the Delphic oracle predict
a fate more horrible than death
      left Corinth, not knowing his origin.
Poor son of Laius, seeing is
believing, but the truth is more blinding than two dress pins.

The more you understand the less you know
for sure what happened. Horrifying things
occurred because of, not despite, his true
      intention to do what was right.
          A feedback of belief and act,
      the self-fulfilling prophecy
reveals two kinds of knowledge, knowledge of what has occurred
and knowledge of intention, which can't always be observed.

I don't know what happened that night
        but nothing came to pass. I left Detroit,
moved to Chicago, never wrote
a book *On God*, forgot about
the incident, and bounced from job
        to job without a clue. Until I came
to California twenty-six
years afterwards, I never thought about my fate again.

But something lingered from that night,
        a vanity that felt like a calling.
Despite the evidence against
the daemon of my teens I still
believed in my most private hour
        that I was meant for something, that somehow
my failures were a test, that things
would finally fall into place when I made my masterpiece.

To be at the beginning once again
and feel the bittersweetness of leaving,
to ride on the Coast Starlight by the sea,
        go fishing in a little skiff
                and contemplate the glassy vast,
        imagine life among sea stacks,
the mount of Morro Rock with its smoldering ash of birds
or turn away for the flintier vistas of Big Sur.

When I arrived in June I went
       straight to the ocean, walked along the pier
and marveled at the freshness of
of its teeming blue vitality.
But I didn't know what to do
       with mountains right against the shore like that
and fog filled every canyon, blocked
the sinuses along the coast like mucus from the flu.

I wandered after work for hours
       up mountains, through the towns and at the beach
to find the sun, which would appear
sometimes, but only as a ghost
through the unknowing June gloom
       to haunt the memory of brighter days.
And then I'd go back to my camp
among the western oaks and stare into the starless dark.

It's dreary to be a stranger again,
to linger in the aisles among the fruits
and vegetables, to study cookie tins
       or cans of soup, look for flip flops
          in the deserted dollar store,
       eat dinner in the parking lot,
and do it all discreetly so as to arouse the least
suspicion of a man in the middle of life alone.

The things our bodies do to stay   3.
       alive and to reproduce don't require
our understanding; things like sleep,
digestion, breathing, pumping blood,
constricting pupils in the light
       or amplifying vibrations to cells
of stereocilia which
transform waves into neural signals to become our words.

I don't know how to extract strength
       from the beef I eat, but I don't need to
in order to enjoy a beef
dipped in jus, topped with peppers hot
and sweet; the pressures of natural
       selection take care of the rest without
my thinking twice about how cells
produce the gastric juices to begin breaking down food.

Almost everything we do we do
for reasons not our own. Even the beef
we favor is a choice we're born into,
       the songs we sing, the words we say,
          the things we live with; changes come
       like accidental variation
and viral replication, differential survival
an all-consuming fire of cultural appropriation.

But what looks like an accident
        is usually someone acting with
a purpose, fueled by a belief
they've found a better way to make
a mousetrap or a government
        through observation, reason, an appeal
to common facts or more abstract
ideas about history and the mind unfolding in time.

So what is the difference between
        a drunken walk and someone looking for
a drink, between a coin toss heads
and the deliberations of
a jury? Does it worry you
        that our intentions might not matter more
to outcomes other than to give
us the illusion that we're masters of our destiny?

Nobody wants to die but it appears
inevitable. People go away
and no one ever hears from them again.
        Sometimes we see their bodies cold
           and stiff like mannequins, the face
        a thin mask of papier mache,
the hands folded mechanically over the sunken chest,
no rise and fall, no falderal, no trace of life at all.

The unknowable pain of death
        must be inferred from other people's deaths.
What was it like before you died?
Were you at peace or terrified?
We can only imagine it.
        We visit the sick to distract them from
their pain and secretly index
their illness to anticipate what might be coming next.

The body tells us everything
        about our own pain. Neurons transmit pain
signals along the axon by
the movement of potassium
and sodium ions in waves
        of depolarization. One by one
action potentials integrate
synaptic messages and propagate them to other cells

until the signals reach the dorsal root
ganglia of a spinal nerve and then
synapse on neurons in the thalamus,
        which relays new information
            to the cerebral cortex where
        the neural impulses are mapped
onto a strange somatosensory homunculus
who speaks in frequencies we learn to interpret in words.

Words that come from the outside world,
       from other people who teach us to turn
our cries into a more refined
description of our pain, through trial
and error, verification
       and validation of how something feels,
or where it hurts and for how long
in an attempt to map the pain from their domain to ours,

which isn't to say there's a name
       for every kind of pain we feel nor that
we've felt the pain of every name
we know, but rather that the names
can act as arrows pointing towards
       recuperation or demise,
a cairn discovered in the wilderness
to focus our attention on finding another sign.

It's difficult to gauge the difference
in our experience of the names of pain.
The signs are the same but the wilderness
       could be altogether different
           like the projection of a sphere
       onto a plane of consciousness.
We talk through differences to bound the gray uncertainty
around a point that feels as far as Alpha Centauri.

After the bonfire of childhood   4.
          belief, a spark remained, despite the ash
of doubt and pain, the de rigeur
rejection of authority,
the existential whiff of white
          suburban privilege and the subsequent
experiments in angst and dread,
the boredom of a lonely evening forced into crisis.

I listened to the arguments
          against religion and conformity,
rejected the mind-body split
but found materialism
inadequate in its account
          of consciousness; experience becomes
belief to keep a thesis up,
whereas belief can be a means to see and understand.

I found myself asleep in Egypt when
my old Greek teacher told me from across
a dark autumn street "the secret of life"
          which I could barely hear because
                    a nervous man was talking as
          we walked into my other ear.
"To talk through… burning with incense… the story… muthos… myth."
A mystery whispered through closed lips. Murmured word of fate.

What is this I, if such there be,
        which day to day continues to exist
amid change and uncertainty,
a control board directing sense
data or simulation for
        the dissipation of ideas, forms,
and energy, the steady creep
of memories, all to propagate the human race?

Or did a demiurge create
        our world for fun? A young Theresa Kim
three hundred years from now computes
a universe with Planck's constant
as her time scale. Arithmetic
        exceeds imagination as the speed
of light is inconceivable.
Genetic algorithms iterate what becomes fate.

We talk and always talk but does it burn?
Something still gnawed at me, a murmured word
of fate abandoned in the wilderness
        until misery brought me face
            to face with the unnameable,
        a memory not quite my own,
a panic of pandemonium. I begged for mercy.
The silence terrified me. But I did survive the night.

On my way home I stopped just east
      of Escalante, Utah on the side
of Highway 12 to take a hike
down a dry wash and look for slot
canyons, arches, and tumbleweeds.
      I had food, water, maps, and the low sun
of mid-November as my guide.
By noon I'd overshot Phipps Arch and came into a floodplain

where I got lost among sagebrush
      and cottonwood, the twisted guts of all
the tributaries turning me
through sandstone canyons and across
the icy Escalante twice
      before I noticed I was going east.
I scrambled up a nameless wash
to look for higher ground and try to make up for lost time.

At two o'clock I could see Highway 12
from Haymaker Bench. I would choose a slot
to get back to the road, then hit a cliff
      and climb back up to look again.
         By five I found myself alone
      and whispering, "Please get me home!"
The day was almost done. The temperature was plummeting
and I might have to shiver the whole night through on the Bench.

For the first time all day I caught
       a signal on my cell, dialed 911,
and someone pointed out the last
canyon before we got cut off.
I made it to the bottom of
       the gulch in total darkness, through the brush,
feeling my way along the walls
until I heard the sound of water rushing by the road.

Here I am in the dark between
       unknowing and knowing my way back home,
between intention and outcome,
a reaching after facts when facts
are nowhere to be found among
       the unobservable quivers of flesh
connecting bone. Ideas reach
into the deep but go no further than words allow.

Only this silence keeps the secret word
transferred from me to you and back again
uncovering a reason to believe
       a random walk in the desert
           will lead, between the flowing stream
       and going home, to destiny:
Remember that you are dust and to dust you shall return
and everything you thought you understood you must unlearn.

"It is what it is" is a motto
 I first heard nearly ten years ago.
"It is what it is," someone said,
 dividing another shit sandwich
 after the boss had gone to bed.
 I liked its fatalism as much
 as the insouciant ricochet
 between Popeye and Yahweh

 and as its usage spread so did
 its intimations range amid
 acceptance and limitation.
 But something changed. "It is" became
 it can only be, impatient
 to move beyond the old refrain
 of "shit happens" and to exclude
 the random from our certitude.

"It is what it is" I now hear
 as an imperative of fear
 as if to say the world is fixed
 and every word is a prison
 in which our feelings contradict
 what it is for what it isn't,
 just another category
 for whatever will be will be.

The expectations are unclear
except in the most general way
but it's impossible to hear
the sun will come again some day

as if the promise of the most
likely event could dissipate
pent-up longings of a morose
adolescent to know the fate

of an unanswered message. Yes
or no may frame uncertainty
but in between you can't suppress
the fragrance of hyperbole.

Statisticians sift exit polls
to divine spite from indifference,
white hot antagonism from cold
numbers, hidden entitlement

from the shrinking middle class,
distinguishing correlation
from causation—did anyone ask
whether the association

of stop and frisk with a decline
in crime implied causation
or do we prefer a hard line?
When the Tiber flooded ancient

Rome, Gallus wanted Tiberius
to consult the Sibylline
books for signs of the mysterious
rains. Preferring to keep divine

things secret, Tiberius demurred.
Like little drops of rain, each vote
precipitates what was inferred:
taxes, Black Lives Matter, turncoat

transgender terrorist event.
The people spoke and we don't want
a pussy for a president.
In the unravelling detente

between parties and among people
we've forgotten how little we know
of ourselves and the sometimes lethal
certainty with which we hallow

an accusation as the truth.
"What is truth?" asked Pontius Pilate
and to avoid being uncouth
left Christ to go take a ballot.

What's true is what happens and what
can be verified by another
but the truth is the cause and nut
of the matter, the uncovered

body of knowledge, transparent
and free, not a commodity,
but immanent and transcendent,
only approached asymptotically.

The polls were right, the race was tight,
and Comey gave enough cover
to the undecided, despite
decency, to rediscover

among hidden variables
a tribal affiliation
to confound the last parable
of civil miscegenation.

And just as raindrops can't conspire
to uncover a levee's flaws,
so great events do not require
the breach of a single great cause.

All summer long the ferns unfurl   1.
their green fringe in the shade.
As daylight starts to wane so does
the dog-day serenade

of a cicada wheezing through
lugubrious afternoons
of adolescence with nowhere
to go and nothing to do.

The summer's over and with it   2.
the dread of its ending.
The lettuces have gone to seed.
But crickets might then sing

into October if the sun
is permitted to shine
and sweeten the split tomatoes
fattening on the vine.

The bright confetti of last night's   3.
sudden gusts through the trees
has settled into a dusting
of honey locust leaves

along the gutters in the crisp
golden light. Blue asters
continue boldly in the cold
of the morning after.

Crows squabble in the canopy   4.
of fiery golden lace;
a leaf falls into the absolute
blue of empty space.

A blush of purple finches on
the wire above the yard,
an embarrassment of riches
for two black cats on guard.

The evenings come quickly now   5.
without an afternoon
and leaves run rattling beneath
the shadows of the moon.

My breath still quickens when an icy
wind begins to rise
and big storms from the north are loosed
to darken once blue skies.

Autumn is a memory palace   6.
of every other fall,
a yellow mat of maple leaves
beyond the garden wall,

another variation of
a lonesome country road
you wandered in the drizzling rain
still golden when it snowed.

The island shifts atop glacial moraines
in the midst of prevailing western winds
across the northern reach of Lake Michigan
where every grain of sand is gathered on
the beach and driven up the windward side
of the dune until they roll down the backslope.
Waves come into the crescent bay like light
in a nineteenth century experiment,
reports of each collapsing edge along
the shore are focused and then amplified
by an amphitheater of sand and stone
before reflecting back to Manitou
Passage. Bearberry and hairy puccoon
and little tufts of creeping juniper
quiver in the foredune. Behind Leland
a streak of peach light peeks through dawn's gray blinds.

The river moves like a conveyor belt
through fields of sugar beets, refineries,
and lumber mills a few inches above
the laminar flow. In the woods, tall oaks
and maples—saplings packed together like
organ pipes in the loft at Holy Cross—
conspire to make dawn gray and dusk charcoal.
Days of rain flood the swales and rot the reeds.
Four dead already this year of heroin.
The chimneys smoke. Cold night. Reluctant spring.
Remembering what it was like and how
it might have been, a country gentleman
wakes at dawn, crosses wetlands, hunts his woods
for turkey, listens for a tom and waits.
Ducks arrow overhead toward Stagg Island.
Coming and going, freighters high and low;
the fishing boats trolling for pickerel fight
the drift like wrappers over a comb plate.

[1]   "Discard anything that does not spark joy." So says Marie
        Kondo. We all know what she means. Get rid of everything
        that does not carry sentiment or that does not give pleasure.
        But joy? Do things give you joy? I like my sweater.
        It's comfortable. It makes me feel confident. Or whatever.
        But it doesn't give me joy.

[2]   Joy can be defined as extreme happiness and pleasure.

[3]   What does your face look like when you are filled with joy?
        Do you want to know?

[4]   How long should joy last? It seems weird to think of joy lasting
        for days like an earache. Joy is a flash. An hour at most.

[5]   A thing of beauty is a joy forever.

[6]   When do we generally first experience joy? Is the joy we
        experience at Christmas the same kind of joy we experience
        as adults? How does time affect our experience of joy?

[7]   Is it better to rarify or normalize joy?

[8]   Joy is a feeling. We have a name for the feeling. We call it joy.

[9]   How can a localized excess of amino acids in a segment of
        DNA be transformed into euphoria? How can cells, synapses,
        and neurotransmitters create the experience of joy?

[10]   When I asked my son when was the last time he experienced
        joy, he told me, "Just now, when I ate that M&M."

[11]   Little boy.

[12]   Full of joy.

[13]   Scarcity vs. abundance.

[14]   Almond Joy.

[15]   Mounds. "Just call it 'Mounds'," I imagine someone saying.

[16]   Must there always be a component of potential with joy? That it can be repeated. Or is this just one axis of joy?

[17]   Swimming in Lake Michigan over deep water where you can still see the bottom of the lake.

[18]   Riding a bike with your shirt off.

[19]   Ode to Joy.

[20]   Is the awareness of joy always retrospective? Some kinds of joy might allow for consciousness of itself while it is happening. But extreme and intense joy; that's hard to be aware of in the moment.

[21]   And if you are able to observe your own joy, how do you do it? Does it make you feel less joy or more if you're aware of it while it's happening?

[22]   When I asked my kids when they first became aware of an experience of joy, they said they couldn't remember ever having an experience like that. Nevertheless, they said they experience joy regularly, like laughter.

[23]   Describe joy succinctly in a few words or a few sentences, as in $F = ma$.

[24]   All art forms attempt to represent joy. But poetry may be the
         least effective art in conveying the feeling of joy. The sheer
         pleasure of color and paint approach exuberance. Some
         descriptions of landscapes or fruit or some other activity might
         be able to convey something similar. But think about music.
         Music can actually make you feel joy. And movies. Remember
         the end of *Breaking Away*. Just as he crosses the finish line
         and raises up his arms in victory. Pure joy. You feel it even in
         watching it. Something about the raising up of arms. The
         connection to the physical. Utterly fleeting.

[25]   The joy of sex. That pretty much covers it.

[26]   Joy is easier to define than shape or color. Less abstract
         than "something bounded."

[27]   "Always rejoice," says Paul, among other things.

[28]   On my way to work I saw a woman jogging. She spread
         her arms apart and smiled in a gesture of joy. Was it the music
         she was listening to? Was she crazy? At the moment of her
         elation, did it matter?

[29]   The axes of joy. Repeatability. Gratuity. Intensity. Perhaps there
         are more.

[30]   At some point, truly intense feeling spills over into physical
         feeling. I suppose "feelings" always have physical manifestations.
         But when I say I'm feeling good, it is unlikely that I am
         referring to anything physical. When I experience joy, however,
         it often has a physical component.

[31]   I asked my daughter if joy can be claimed. She said, "No, joy
         happens. You can't claim it; you can only receive it."

[32]   Thus says the Lord, according to the prophet Zechariah,
        "Rejoice heartily, o daughter Zion, shout for joy,
        o daughter Jerusalem."

[33]   The imperative to rejoice is common in many religions.
        I mention this observation to my wife, who is not religious. I'm
        Catholic. She is careful to point out that joy is not the
        exclusive domain of religion. But I'm not suggesting as much,
        despite atheists being such a dour self-satisfied bunch. I'm
        kidding! Atheists are hilarious. Most of my friends are atheists
        or agnostics. And I certainly have shared many non-religious
        joys with my wife. I've also experienced religious joys with
        her—the events may be the same, but we understand them
        differently. The birth of our children is an obvious example. But
        I'm simply noting that joy and suffering are frequently paired,
        especially in a religious context, as if you can't have one without
        the other. And in the case of many saints, such as St. Teresa,
        suffering leads directly to joy, even to ecstasy.

[34]   "More than that, we rejoice in our sufferings, knowing that
        suffering produces endurance, and endurance produces
        character, and character produces hope, and hope does not
        disappoint us, because God's love has been poured into
        our hearts through the Holy Spirit who has been given to us."
        Romans 5:3-5.

[35]   I first heard Beethoven's Ninth when I was 14 and saw
         A Clockwork Orange. While I neither identified with Alex nor with
         the feelings Beethoven stirred in him—specifically the
         compulsion to violence—I was possessed by the Ninth, even
         listening to a few notes. The tingling began at the back of my
         head and worked its way down my spine and into my limbs. The
         first time I heard it live, I convulsed in my seat, amplifying
         the vibrations I felt through the floor. Whenever I went to hear
         the Ninth again, I made sure to find an edge seat, high in
         the balcony so no one would notice me trembling. Was that joy
         or possession? At what point does joy become ecstasy?

[36]   We retain our sense of self in joy, but we lose it in ecstasy.

[37]   Joy arises from a physical feeling or induces a physical feeling.
         A tingling at the base of the neck. Tears. A lump in the throat.

[38]   A while back I accepted a job offer and met my new bosses for
         dinner several weeks before I started. I was leaving structural
         engineering for quantitative analysis, a field about which I knew
         next to nothing. I had spent almost a decade focusing on seismic
         analysis and design of nuclear power plants. Challenging and
         often stressful, the work was made more demanding by the fact
         that I worked for assholes. Big-time, greedy, duplicitous assholes.
         But the US nuclear industry was and is dying and because
         of the highly specialized skill set required to do the work, it can
         be very difficult to get out. I had spent years applying to other
         jobs both inside and outside of the industry and I knew the
         transition to becoming a quant was a longshot at best. So when

I confirmed over the course of dinner that not only had I gotten out of the nuclear industry but that I may have landed a good job working with good people, I felt a little giddy, like I had managed through persistence and serendipity to escape a high-security prison. The night was bitterly cold. Although my feet were frozen as I rode my bike home I found myself laughing spontaneously. I knew I didn't deserve my new job, but I didn't care. That's what I mean by the gratuity of joy.

[39]   A few years ago I was on a six-month field assignment at a nuclear power plant on the central coast of California, about halfway between San Francisco and Los Angeles. My family came out from Chicago and stayed with me for a month in Morro Bay. On the final weekend of their visit we drove down to LA, which was apparently in the midst of a heat wave, 93° and dry. Admittedly the bungalow we rented near Chinatown was a little hot, so we drove to Venice Beach for a swim. The water was temperate and the waves were sublime. We played in the surf until the sun went down. At one point in the late afternoon I was about fifty yards out from where my wife and kids were swimming. I caught the crest of a particularly shapely wave and felt a surge of water buoy me to the surface, my head haloed in foam. The wave was hurtling me straight towards my family when both of my kids noticed. They told me I reminded them of the river dragon in *Spirited Away*, that I had become all wave but for a floating head. And that's exactly how I felt, like a fucking sea dragon. At the beach with my family. Wave after wave.

[40]   What does it mean to claim joy? Perhaps the deepest joy is born of suffering, suffering that teaches us to give up expectations, that insists on the virtue of acceptance.

[41]   Only when your expectations are stripped away do you begin to
         appreciate how little you deserve, that despite your decency
         and hard work and commitment to whatever you consider to be
         virtuous causes, there are billions of people just as deserving
         of validation as you and many no doubt are more deserving.
         But this is not an admonition to appreciate growing up in a
         wealthy country. Nor is this a denial of basic human rights. This
         is just what suffering teaches.

[42]   Many different kinds of suffering afflict us, including physical
         and psychological suffering. Chronic disease brings physical
         pain and discomfort as well as psychological suffering. While
         physical pain can be seen as a mental interpretation of physical
         stimuli, the suffering has an organic basis, whereas psychological
         suffering is based entirely on an interpretation of events.
         In the case of disease, you might fear death or worry that your
         physical condition won't improve, which leads to a sense of
         hopelessness. "It's never going to get better."

[43]   Most people, even most Christians, regard the emphasis
         on suffering found in Kierkegaard and Dostoevsky as too heavy
         and needlessly ghoulish. And if it was presented as an alien
         theology, most people would utterly reject all that misery and
         misunderstanding. Why so much suffering and sacrifice? From
         a certain perspective the New Testament can seem not only
         absurd, but inhuman. Love your enemies, always rejoice,
         especially when you're miserable. Why? Certainly some martyrs
         took pleasure in pain, but let's set aside the perverse for a
         moment, to see if there is a theological point to all of this
         suffering. According to the Gospels, the parables are not enough
         to get people to see. Miracles are not enough. Healing is not
         enough. Even when Jesus enters Jerusalem and is greeted as the
         Messiah, his kingdom is completely misunderstood. And in
         Mark, which originally ended with Mary Magdalene, Mary, and
         Salome fleeing an empty tomb in terror, even the risen
         Christ is confounding. So what's it going to take? "Take up your

cross and follow me." I don't like the sound of it either. It seems joyless and humorless. But then you get the resurrection.

[44] Of all the things he could've done after the resurrection, Jesus chose to barbecue. What could be more beautiful than grilling fishes at the beach for your friends? The affirmation of fishes and loaves, the most basic meal.

[45] At the end of *It's a Wonderful Life* George Bailey runs down the street affirming the very shittiness of the life he's been trying to escape. Yes. That's claiming joy. Claiming joy in the shabby and mundane. And the only way to that joy is through a vision of suffering and death.

[46] I get why Nietzsche raged against Christianity. It's a crazy religion. And he probably was more than a bit of an asshole himself. But the things that seem so distasteful—sin and suffering and repentance—are also what most resonate with experience. And the unprovable articles of faith like the incarnation, the resurrection, and the trinity align in such perfect syzygy that they radiate the truth like the coronal filaments of a total eclipse.

[47] Does that last line make you uncomfortable? Too poetic? Too naive? As in, "this guy is a creepy Christian?" Consider Euclid's parallel postulate. From this apparently self-evident assertion, that parallel lines remain parallel all the way out to infinity, you get Euclidean geometry and a wealth of geometric facts that can be put to practical use in, for example, the design of nuclear power plants. For over two thousand years people went on doing geometry until Lobachevsky came along and showed that the parallel postulate was an axiomatic assumption, an article of faith if you will. We can barely walk without making assumptions. Some of them are explicit, others are hidden. And still others we pretend are laws as inevitable as gravity.

[48]   But they are only laws until they are unproven by irreconcilable
         observations.

[49]   Back to definitions. Hunger, torture, these seem like the worst
         kinds of suffering. To be tortured to death for a crime you
         did not commit, for no crime at all, that seems like the bottom
         of misery and injustice, whether you believe or not. In the
         silence before dying, the wrongfully accused must realize, "This
         is it. This is how it's going to happen. Life is truly not fair."

[50]   Now back to psychological suffering. What is the source of
         our suffering? In the simplest terms, suffering is wanting
         something and not getting it. Suffering is to want something
         badly and still not get it. Even when we are sick and in pain, we
         seek relief more than anything. When we cannot obtain that
         relief we suffer. One remedy for suffering is to snuff out our
         desires. But there is another way, which is to learn to live with
         our desires and the disappointment associated with them.
         But what does such disappointment show us? Above all, that
         justice is not comprehensible.

[51]   I want to leave this place. I want some respect. I want to love
         somebody, really love somebody. I want to be loved. I just want
         some fucking money. Suffering teaches us drop by drop the
         vanity of our wishes and the essence of our needs. So to rejoice
         in suffering, to claim joy in the everyday, that is affirmation.

[52]   I have a friend from college who spent the last three years in
         prison for organizing a protest against the Venezuelan
         government. He went home this summer to his family under
         house arrest. It's been ten years since I've had any contact with
         him. One of the most grueling and saddest experiences
         I've had to endure is being away from my family for six months
         out in California. When I wasn't working, I found it hard not

to always think of home, even as I was swimming among the
sea lions. Leo has two young kids he hadn't seen in three years.
I thought of him often during his imprisonment, trying to
imagine what it was like. At some point he must have
considered that it would all end badly. But the joy of going
home! That you get to eat dinner with your family again. And
tomorrow night, after another day has passed, you get to eat
together again.

[53]   Sometimes the damage from suffering is permanent. Sometimes
there is no going home.

[54]   I have a little vegetable garden in my backyard where I grow
peppers and tomatoes and herbs of every kind. It pleases
me to watch the bees battling for the lavender. Sometimes when I
study the tomatoes fattening on the vine, the pleasure of
anticipation is so deep, it would be better to call the pleasure joy.

[55]   DJ Khaled in his yard where he praises a purple flower
and the lemons on his lemon tree. Has anybody seen this? It's
like St. Francis's "Canticle of the Sun." I love you.

[56] Joy is a cluster of feelings gathered around the axes of
anticipation/repetition, intensity (usually physical), and gratuity
through suffering. There is a fourth dimension of joy. The joy of
freedom. My last month in California I worked the night shift.
From 6 pm to 6 am every day for 22 days in a row I sat in a
double-wide trailer next to the ocean reviewing calculations and
listening to Lester Young. I just couldn't get enough of
his sound. At 9 pm and at 3 am I had to climb into a hatch and
inspect the construction of my design. Nodding at the crew,
I checked out some rebar splices, waved, and left the way I
came. At 6 am, I briefed my replacement and went back to my
apartment in San Luis Obispo, which was entirely empty except
for a sleeping bag, a spoon, a bowl, and a cup, two books,
and two boogie boards I bought when my family was staying out
there with me. I would wake up just after noon and eat a bowl
of cereal on the floor as the sun blazed into the empty living
room. I loved that sunshine. By 2 pm I'd be back at the
beach with my boogie board, where I might see a surfer or two.
Often I showered at the beach and went straight to work.
I spoke to almost no one during those three weeks, just the
foreman and the day-shift engineer. I was like a monk devoted
to the ocean; the waves were my offices. It was lonely but I got
used to it. On my last day at the plant I went back to the
day shift and came to work with all my belongings. Before going
home I had to drive down to Newport Beach for a weeklong
conference on seismic risk assessment, but basically I was done.
My design had been successfully built and I was going home.
As I left the plant and drove along the ocean, I suppose the
anticipation of going home buoyed me, but the clean break felt
sweeter, even joyous. As much as I came to love that coast,
and I still think about those waves every day, there is an inexpres-
sible joy to leaving, especially when everything is buttoned
up. The feeling is fleeting, one free of anticipation or obligation.
The feeling is the feeling of freedom. And I felt it on Highway
101 driving down to LA.

[57] During spring migration this year, I was able to stop by the Magic Hedge at Montrose Beach to look at birds nearly every morning. One especially bright day in mid-May, I stood next to two dudes with big cameras hanging from their necks. We had just seen a Connecticut warbler skulking in the brush and they began high-fiving each other. I overheard that they had flown all the way from California just for two days at the Hedge. And the Connecticut was giving them what they came for. I waited by a tangle of honeysuckle as most birders moved on. With only a few minutes left before I had to head to work I noticed nearly a dozen female redstarts making the quietest titter in the bush. Although they were darting from branch to branch apparently braiding unseen dimensions of air, they never left the honeysuckle. Bathed in such dewy light, everything about them seemed new and fresh. It was like standing at the gates of paradise. And where was I going? In or out?

Acknowledgments

"Notes on Joy" first appeared in *Obsidian* as a part of
"Experiments in Joy," an ongoing poetics project in which Black
artists and their allies are invited to share reflections and
artworks. The author wishes to thank editor and poet Duriel E.
Harris for the invitation and encouragement to participate.
"Out West" first appeared in *Aurochs*. "Bound Away," "Escape to
Alcatraz," and "Sunrise Over South Manitou Island"
first appeared in *Hampden-Sydney Poetry Review*.

Finally, the author wishes to thank Joel Felix, Devin Johnston,
and Peter O'Leary for their suggestions and encourage-
ment regarding these poems and to Philip Burton for the design
of the book.

About the author

Michael O'Leary is the author of *The Reception*. He started off
his career in data entry, but soon left for landscaping and
construction, then became a jazz record auctioneer as well as a
shelver of books at the local research library, which led to
a stint as a grant writer at a university where he met a titan of
industry and became a ghost writer. Somewhat desperate for a
stable income, O'Leary became an engineer in the nuclear
power industry. When the bottom fell out, he landed in a career
as a quantitative analyst in the financial services industry.
All of this occurred over the course of thirty years in Chicago
where he still lives. He is an editor for Flood Editions in
his free time.